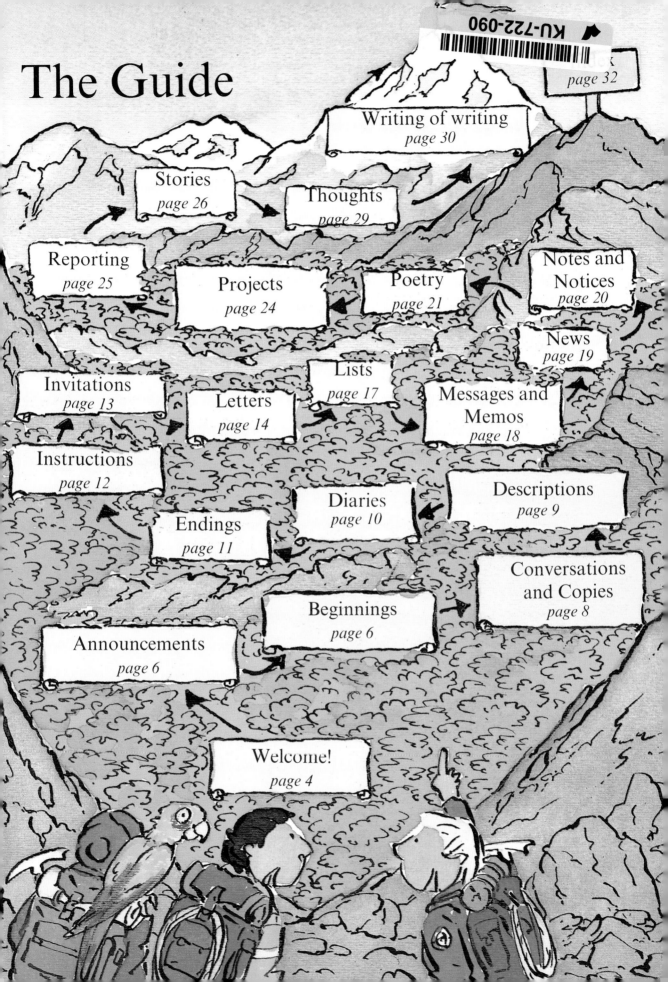

The Guide

page 32

Writing of writing
page 30

Stories
page 26

Thoughts
page 29

Reporting
page 25

Projects
page 24

Poetry
page 21

Notes and Notices
page 20

News
page 19

Invitations
page 13

Letters
page 14

Lists
page 17

Messages and Memos
page 18

Instructions
page 12

Descriptions
page 9

Endings
page 11

Diaries
page 10

Conversations and Copies
page 8

Announcements
page 6

Beginnings
page 6

Welcome!
page 4

Welcome!

Welcome to the world of writing!

Good writing is just like exploring. Good writers need courage, good ears, good eyes and good minds. Then, if they have something to write with and something to write on, the world is theirs. There are so many paths to take with so many people, places and times to meet.

Writing....

to please
to complain
to explain
to find out
to tell
to let others know
to remember
to get things done
to congratulate
to know
to thank
to console
to put down thoughts
to warn
to record or
to put the record straight
to entertain and make laughter
to plan
to imagine
to order
out of duty
to spread news
for friends
for everyone
to express feelings
for fun
private writing

Exploring the ways of writing is not always easy. It can be an uphill struggle with disappointments and dead ends. Some people love it much more than others. We all live in the world of writing. It is for us to make use of, to enjoy, to share and to explore.

Fun with English

Good Writing

WILLIAM EDMONDS

The author wishes to express his particular
gratitude to Robert Wheeler, the designer of all the
books in this series. There has been an especially
close collaboration at every stage and the author
has found this an immense stimulus and
encouragement. The author would also like to
thank Terry McKenna for his superbly amusing
illustrations, invaluable ingredients of the series.
William Edmonds wishes to thank Karen
Wilbraham who collaborated with him in the
planning and writing of this book.

KINGFISHER
Kingfisher Publications Plc
New Penderel House, 283–288 High Holborn,
London WC1V 7HZ

The material in this edition was previously published
by Kingfisher Publications Plc in the *Wordmaster* series
(1993) and in the *Guide to Good English* series (1989)

This edition published by Kingfisher Publications Plc 1999
10 9 8 7 6 5 4 3 2 1
1TR/0399/EDK/(ATL)/140EDI

This edition copyright © Kingfisher Publications Plc 1995
Text copyright © William Edmonds 1989
Illustrations copyright © Kingfisher Publications Plc
1989, 1993

A CIP catalogue record for this book is available from
the British Library

ISBN 0 7534 0370 6

Printed in Spain

Exciting times for writing

These are now exciting times for writing. There are so
many gadgets and machines to help us write, from all
kinds of pencils and pens to typewriters, computers,
copiers and so on. There are also machines that save us
from writing such as telephones, recording machines,
cameras, televisions and so on. Will writing die out and
someday be taken over by new inventions altogether?

But not to worry! The world is more full of writing than
ever before. Each year the numbers of books, papers
and amounts of writing multiply. More and more
people are writing and we seem to be writing even more
and more. Writing is certainly here to stay for a good
while.

Writing to save time

Can this be so? Surely it is easier and quicker to say
words than to write them. Yes it is, but spoken words
usually disappear for ever. If you write them down the
words are saved for as long as you like. And anyway
most of us can read them much faster than we can speak
them. Not only can writing save ideas and news, it can
also play with them, imagine them or plan them.
Writing saves all kinds of time.

Talking Time
This book now takes us on a grand exploration of many
of the ways of writing. Good writing can be catching. It
will easily spread and go to your head. But it always
takes time. So Take Care and Good Luck!

Announcements

Congratulations to all readers of this book. You have embarked on an exciting mission.

Passengers are advised that the next voyage to the unknown will start at midnight

Mr and Mrs Brer Rabbit would like to announce the birth of four sweet bunnies.

These are short easy ways of making information, intentions or feelings known. We all have special announcements to make at times. Try putting one on the door of your room and see if anybody takes notice.

Beginnings

How shall we begin? Oh dear! I don't know what to write first. I'm afraid of spoiling the nice clean page. Oh! Panic stations! Let's have a cup of coffee instead.

Coffee for beginners

Many writers say they feel like this before they start working. Beginnings can be the hardest part of writing.

Here are a few ways of helping to get started:

● Try a practice start. Put down all your first ideas quickly without worrying about the order, spelling, handwriting, etc. Then play around with them and use the best bits for a real start. But don't forget you can always change it again later.

6

- Start with a bold simple title:

PARROTS

- Follow with a general statement on what you are writing about.

   Parrots can be very puzzling.

- Use a traditional opening.

   Once upon a time ...
      There was once ...

- Set the scene (give an idea of the time and place of what you are writing about).

When I was on my way to school last Friday ...

- Start dramatically:

'Bang!' – the door slammed and Sally was left alone with a bucket stuck to her right foot, clutching the frightened pink rabbit.

- Begin with a few words that create a special atmosphere of expectation:

It was a dark and stormy night ...
Deep, deep in the forest ...
Where is the green parrot?
The Iron Man came to the top of the hill ...

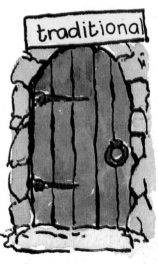

- Remember that the first words are really like an advertisement for all the writing that is to follow. They have to be enticing.

You have no excuses now –
pick up your pen and write!

Copies

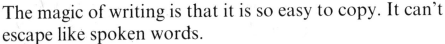

The magic of writing is that it is so easy to copy. It can't escape like spoken words.

For a special piece of writing it is sometimes necessary to make two or three different copies before you can get it just as you want it. Good writers are never afraid to keep on making changes.

The Intrepid Explorers

The three explorers set off on a mission to reach the top of the world. They took a large map and some secret instructions and a hefty supply of baked beans.

The Intrepid Explorers
On Friday the first of June the three explorers set off from Brighton on a mission to reach the top of the world. They took a large map, some secret instructions, and a hefty supply of baked beans.

Once you have done all your changes then you can use a printer or a photo-copier to make as many samples of the final draft as you like.

Conversations

"Mum, I don't want to go to school," said Tom.
"You know you have to go," replied his mother.
"But the children dislike me and so do the teachers," moaned Tom.
"Tom don't be so silly, you have to go, you're the Headmaster," said his mother.

We have special ways of showing speech in writing. We use a type of punctuation called speech marks ("" or ' ') which we put at the beginning and the end of the actual words that are being spoken. We also always start a new line each time somebody new is speaking.

Descriptions

Descriptions are like pictures. They are ways of using words to give an idea of what a person, place or event is like. Sometimes we need good descriptions so that we can identify somebody or something we are looking for.

Descriptions can be used to make writing more interesting. We can say

The door closed.

or we give more detail and say

The old red wooden door swung on its rusty hinges and closed with an ominous creak.

WANTED

Female – aged 200 years. 3 metres tall with a pink and green hairstyle. Last seen in the middle of the North sea wearing orange trousers and a shiny green jumper. WARNING – Do not approach this woman – but contact your local Police Station

---

Can you add descriptions to make these sentences more interesting?

Jane went down the road.
The dog barked.

What's this?
An enormous four-footed animal. It has a very, very long nose which it uses like a hand to pick up things . It has big floppy ears and is usually grey.

Answer – An elephant

Try giving a description of an animal or an object to your friend, without using your hands. Can they guess what you mean?

Diaries

Writing a diary is usually a personal matter. It's a way of recording events and personal thoughts. It can be like having a conversation with yourself.

Monday 6th February Mum says if I don't tidy up my bedroom she is going to stop my pocket money for five weeks.

Tuesday 7th February Dad has sided with mum. At this rate I won't get any pocket money for another 3 years.

Wednesday 8th February I decided I might as well give in and tidy. By bedtime I had only got as far as crawling under my bed. I found an apple core, 3 odd socks, my best catapult, an old shoe and two years of my favourite comics.

Thursday 9th February Dad says it's all going into the bin if I don't do something before the Friday deadline. I moved around a few boxes but it didn't convince mum.

Friday 10th February Things are getting really bad – I think I might have to run away. Even my teacher says I'm untidy – he made me stay in at playtime and clean my desk. I told him that brilliant people are always untidy but I don't think he believed me.

> **Saturday 11th February** Gave in and tidied up (just hope they don't look in my wardrobe)— now it doesn't even look like my room. When I'm grown up I'll remember this. If I ever have any children I'll allow them to be brilliant and untidy.

> **Sunday 12th February** Too exhausted from tiding up to do or write anything.

It's fun keeping your own diary. Try writing one in a notebook. Enjoy using it – but only when you have got something to say – otherwise it might become a chore. Think of a diary as a secret friend – but remember to keep it in a safe place!

Endings

Endings are important as they are the last words and thoughts that a reader is left with.

"They came to the river, they came to the bridge – they crossed it hand in hand – then over the hills and far away she danced with Pigling Bland!"

(From *The Tale of Pigling Bland* by Beatrix Potter, © Frederick Warne & Co., 1913, 1987.)

Endings can be neatly finished off –

. . . and so they all lived happily ever after.

– or they can leave us to decide our own conclusions, allowing us to complete the story as we want to. This is called an open ending.

and so they came to the top of the hill. They looked about them and wondered where they would go next.

THE END

Instructions

Instructions tell you how to make or do something. Often there are diagrams to help, that go with the writing. It is usually a good idea to list the instructions in careful order.

1 Take a rectangular piece of paper and fold it in half in line with the longer side. Then unfold it again so that you can see the crease.

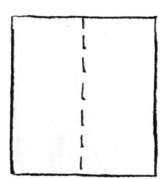

2 Now fold the top two corners to meet the middle crease.
. . . .

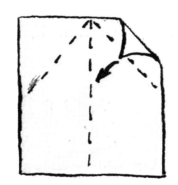

Can you complete these instructions so that you are finished with a good design? Or perhaps you could write instructions on how to make one of your favourite meals, a bed, a surprise or even a mess?

HOW TO CROSS THE QUICK SANDS
Strap boards onto feet
Follow the red arrows
Never stop still!

Instructions always need to be followed carefully stage by stage. It is very easy to get them wrong. So it is best to make them as simple and as straightforward as possible.

Invitations

Invitations ask you to attend an event. It is best to make them look bright, colourful and inviting.

COME TO A PARTY

Julie invites you to her birthday party on 3rd June

5pm ~ 9pm

R.S.V.P

R.S.V.P. stands for *Répondez s'il vous plaît* the French for *reply if you please*.

> So how about having a party and making some invitations?

Jokes

There was a parrot who liked writing
Especially about something exciting
He flew into the air
And hijacked a bear
Now isn't that something worth writing?

Often we think that writing has to be a serious business and that it is always hard work. Give up that idea. *Righting* is far more fun than fighting. It's almost as delightful as writing (GROAN!).

13

Letters

There are many different reasons for writing letters.
Some we do out of duty:

29 December

24 Royal Road
Crabtree
Yorkshire
TLN 4EP

Dear Uncle Fred,
                    Thank you very much for giving me
your old school tie for Christmas. The colours of
orange, yellow and red will go very well with my
new green shirt and dad says it will prove
very useful.

I hope you had a good Christmas with aunt
May and uncle Joe. By the way, did you give
Cousin Rosie an old school tie as well?

Hope you are fit and well. Once again thank you,

Your loving nephew,
                    Ben

I can't ever imagine receiving a worse present-mean old so and so! What revolting colours but I'd better humour the old chap.

Sometimes we have to write letters like this because it is the polite thing to do. We have to try and please the person we are writing to. It is best to try and make it fun rather than a chore. There is a set way of presenting your letter with, for example, the address on your right (as shown above).

There are non-personal letters that you need to write for more formal reasons, such as to do with business.

In this case it is important to lay out the beginning and end of your letter in the customary way, including adding the name and address of the company or department you are writing to:

---

24 Royal Road,
Crabtree,
Yorkshire
TLN 4EP

Fun Travel Ltd.,
22 Back Street,
Bristol
BR 2GA

23rd February 1990

Dear Sir or Madam,

I have read about your special fun holidays in the African Jungle. I enclose a stamped addressed envelope and would be pleased if you could send me a free brochure with details of cheap fares for sensible children.

Yours faithfully,

Ann Jones

Ms Ann Jones

When we are writing formal letters to people we don't know at all it is usual to end with *Yours faithfully* or *Yours truly*. If we know who the person is then it is best to use his or her name (Dear Ms Smith) and conclude with *Yours sincerely*.

Try looking through the magazines and see if there is anything interesting to send away for, or even complain about. Set out your letter like the one here.

There are also friendly letters that we really enjoy writing and receiving – chatty letters to friends, for instance.

My Place
Sat night

Dear Clare,
          Hello - sorry it's so long since I've written but I have been very busy My cat has had kittens - they are so cute - the smallest one is ginger and white and so naughty! I hope your mum and dad let you come to stay and then you can come and see them.
     Last week I got my photos back from the holiday - there are some really good ones of you in the pool. I'm putting one in the envelope for you.
     I hope school is okay - we are doing a really boring topic at the moment - on butterflies again - would you believe it!

     Write back soon
          Love Sue ×××

fan letters

love letters

enquiry letters

Letters to friends are often like a written telephone conversation (and usually much cheaper) and do not have to be 'correct' English. They can be very chatty and lots of fun to read and write. So next time you have a chance, pen a few lines to a friend, or even to your old granny on her own. Enjoy it!

complaining letters

congratulations letters

apology letters

Lists

Friends and phone numbers
Sally 343434
Sunita 29642
Mick and Shirley 185634
Jin Hee 123456
Angela 654321

Shopping
sugar
eggs
biscuits
jam
honey
bread
milk
coffee

Menu
Soup 50p
Sausage, beans and chips £1.20
Fish and chips £1.40
Hamburger 90p
Cheeseburger £1
Hot Dog 60p
Tea   25p
Coffee   30p

Reminders
feed the cat
Hang out the washing
fetch the paper
Phone Fred
Prepare tea

What I want for Xmas
New bike   Football kit
A computer   Sweets

Favourite footballers or popstars
_____
_____
_____
_____
_____

Spellings
knee
key
knife
comb
bomb
gnome
tongue
sign

Messages and Memos

> IMPORTANT!!
> Must remember to collect the cat from the vet at 5pm

> HELP!
> I'm stranded on a desert Island

These are the kinds of messages that we usually write on scraps of paper to remind ourselves or to tell our friends simple bits of information, requests or maybe endearments. They are really little letters passed around in an informal way.

People who work in offices are always sending messages to each other and they usually call these memos (memoranda). They have a correct way of doing them to make sure there is no misunderstanding.

MEMO

TO _Jane Smith_   DATE _3rd June_

FROM _Sally White_   TIME _4 pm_

MESSAGE _Could you find out all the details from the Wilson's file?_

News

Latest News

EXPLORERS IN NARROW ESCAPE

Three explorers and a parrot yesterday narrowly escaped being buried in an avalanche. They had just successfully crossed the dangerous quicksands to reach the mountains when they heard an almighty rumbling from above. Not a moment too soon . . . (continued on page 3)

Teachers tighten rules
Anybody found running in the corridors will in future be punished severely. The headmaster went blue in the face as he said "This is the very last warning . . ."

Ringmer School Football Team win Tournament
On Saturday our team won 5 out of the 6 matches to become the district champions. Our player of the tournament was Neil who saved the day with his brilliant goalkeeping.

Newspapers and news-sheets are an excellent way of making use of good writing. We all like to read the latest news. Journalists, the people who write newspapers, have particular ways of writing which easily catch attention. Snappy headlines are a good idea as well as short sharp sentences.

Computers (especially with desktop publishing programs) and photocopiers make the production of newspapers quite easy.

The fastest known speed is the speed of light. Light travels at 299,792.5 kilometres per second. Scientists have discovered that light always travels through space at exactly that speed. It never goes faster or slower.

Notes

Notes are usually a shortened form of writing. A short letter or message is sometimes called a note. But we also talk of making notes when we mean making a shortened form of something which is said or written.

Note-making or note-taking is a useful skill that allows us to keep a brief written record of anything we want.

When somebody is speaking, it is impossible to write down every word but we can just write a few words to indicate the main points that are being made.

> light has fastest speed – 299,792.5 km per sec, never changes

We usually write such notes just for ourselves so they don't have to be in correct English as long as they make sense to us.

Notes can also be made from a piece of writing that we want to shorten or we want to remind ourselves of.

NB (Please Note) Good note-making pays off.

Notices

NETBALL TEAM FOR SATURDAY

C J. Wright   GK K. Long
WA P. Lemon   GD P. Cass
WD F Sharp
GA L. Pine

IMPORTANT – meet at 9am at school

Notices are a way of spreading information. They are usually put up in an obvious place such as a noticeboard. Have you any notices on your wall?

Poetry

Poetry is poetry
It may be good
It may be bad
It may be happy
It may be sad.

Some like poetry
Some detest it
Some write it beautifully
By now you must have guessed it.

(Peter, aged 9, from *Young Writers Young Readers*,
reprinted by permission of Boris Ford, the editor.)

Poems are like people – they can come in any size, shape
or form. Writing poetry is different from other kinds of
writing because it allows us to play with words in just
the way we like. We can even bend the normal ways of
grammar, change spellings or even make new words and
sounds.

Gust Becos I Cud Not Spel

Gust becos I cud not Spel
It did not mean I was daft
When the boys in school red my riting
Some of them laffed.

("Gargling with Jelly" by Brian Patten
from *Gargling with Jelly*, © Brian Patten, 1985.
Published by Viking Kestrel and in Puffin Books.)

The great thing about poems is that you can control them just how you like. They can never be wrong. What is more, a poem can be your thoughts on paper about anything you choose.

Mum and dad feeling mad,
Little me feeling sad.

Just take the words and line by line,
Think of things you want to say,
Then rearrange and play and play.
Until at last it sounds just right,
Then read it aloud or hide it out of sight.

It is important to remember that poems do not have to rhyme. They can also pay attention to the sound patterns in other ways. For instance poetry can follow a strict and regular rhythmic pattern.

Breathless
(written at 21,200 feet on May 23rd)

Heart aches,
Lungs pant,
The dry air
Sorry, scant.
Legs lift
And why at all?
Loose drift,
Heavy fall.
Prod the snow
Its easiest way;
A flat step,
Is holiday.

(From "Breathless" by Wilfrid Noyce;
reprinted by permission of Wm. Heinemann, Ltd.)

This poem can give us the feeling of the steady rhythm of climbing the mountain. The short lines help show the breathlessness.

You can write poems about places you have visited, things you have seen, things that have happened to you, and those created by your imagination. Anytime you think of a few words you like jot them down in a notebook and you can use some of them in a poem later.

lorries -tigers
roaring / hot breath
fumes -jungle of
colours -people /
insects scurry-
ing — houses /
trees / towering

The tiger lorries roared passed
The hot fume breath misted the air.
Out of control they raced down the hill,
Dodging in and out,
Miraculously missing the scurrying people
Reds, greens, purples, oranges, yellows,
Gay and gaudy amongst the brick grey
    and concrete jungle.
The chattering motorbikes-screaming,
To a halt at the traffic lights
Animal like obeying the jungle law.

You can draft (rewrite) your poem as many times as you like, until you get one poem or several poems that you are happy with.

So, poetry is poetry – you can make it do what you like. Try it and see for yourself. You can never go wrong.

Projects

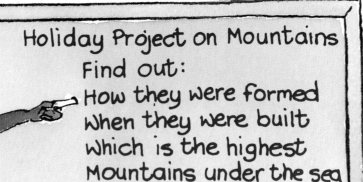

Holiday Project on Mountains
Find out:
How they were formed
When they were built
Which is the highest
Mountains under the sea
Mountain wildlife
Mountain climbers
What are volcanoes

Doing a project in school usually involves finding out and collecting information about a particular subject, be it dinosaurs, explorers or parrots. The basic meaning of the noun *project* is actually *a plan*. Doing a good project therefore depends on making good plans. One way to start is to make a list of questions about what you might want to find out:

Where do parrots come from?
What are the best-known parrots?
Where do they naturally make their nests?
Is it cruel to keep them as pets?
How are they tamed? etc. . . . .

Information books and encyclopedias will help you get started, but accounts of any first-hand experience that you or any of your friends may have will make it much more interesting. Projects are also good opportunities for making models and pictures, but it is your own writing which will bring them all together.

Reporting

Putting it down in writing: this is what we do when we want words to really stick. There are many occasions when we do this.

School Report

Name: *Edward Lock* Class: *2W*

Subject	Grade	Comment
English	B	He is lively in oral work but lacks concentration in writing
Mathematics	C	Could do better.

REPORT OF NATURE CLUB
On Friday 24ᵗʰ April the nature club went for a ramble through the woods. They saw carpets of bluebells, two squirrels playing on an oak tree and a stray parrot. Everybody wondered where the parrot had come from.

Agreement
I promise to pay Thomas £2 for cleaning my car
Signed   Date

Once any kind of written record is made it can be seen or examined by anyone and at any time. This kind of writing needs to be done with care. To help us there are often set ways of doing them. The best reports are fair and not too long. As we shall see next, a report about something that has happened can also be a good story.

Swimming Certificate

This is to certify that

Susan Lock

has swum 200 metres breaststroke.

Date: Signed

26·7·89   D. Gardner

Stories

Everyday stories

"Do you know what happened last night! I had just finished my tea and was looking out of the window when I saw this strange thing moving along the garden fence. I went outside and saw this amazing bird...."

Stories all the time

They go on anywhere and everywhere. Everything that happens makes a story – it only needs someone to tell it. In fact, most of us are bursting with stories all the time just from our everyday lives:

What happened?

Last night? On Saturday morning? Just now? During the holidays? At breakfast? Under the bed? At the end of the garden? At your gran's? To the cat? When you were much younger? On that day you will never forget? And whenever and wherever you have been?

Every story is special

Stories grow from gossip. Sometimes the same story gets better and better with each telling. Sometimes, too, we can make them really good by taking the trouble to write them down. We then have to choose the bits of the story that matter most to us. Each story-teller or writer has her or his own way of doing this. That's what makes stories fun to read. We know that each one is going to be different.

Is there a special way of writing everyday stories? Not really. It is probably best first to write the story just as it comes to you. You may find that you get carried away with it. Let that happen and then afterwards look at it as a reader and you may want to trim it or check the sentences. Then polish the beginning and ending.

26

Imagined Stories

As everybody knows, *telling stories* does not necessarily mean telling the truth. If you get fed up with trying to tell ordinary stories, it can be fun, for a change, to tell a story made from the most deliberate lies that you can think of.

> Bobby pulled at the bucket on his foot but it was well and truly stuck. The telephone rang, he leapt up, slid on the floor and fell on the cream trifle. Just at that moment his Mum got home from work.
> "I can explain, honestly," stuttered Bobby.

But most made-up stories have some truth in them, usually to do with feelings, such as of sadness, fear, worry, excitement, joy, or whatever. If you try writing about a lonely pig you will find yourself writing about what you know personally about loneliness. Good fairy-tales do just this kind of thing and that is why they are so popular and so satisfying to write.

> See what truths you discover if you write about *The Sad Banana, The Silly Sausage, The Greedy Grasshopper, The Angry Ant, The Unhappy Elephant, The Lazy Lollipop, The Ugly Duckling* or about things or creatures of a special nature.

Horrors, especially, can make spellbinding stories.

> Amelia sat up in bed quickly. Something had woken her, she knew it wasn't normal. The rain tried to get in her window, the wind moaned her name and Amelia clutched her teddy tightly and waited . . .

Stories in any shape or size

Round stories

boring. ...Andy fell asleep. He dreamed

Tall stories

Did I ever tell
you about the time
I saw a pig fly?
Well, it was one
of those funny days
in summer when
everywhere is hazy
with heat. I was
having an argument
with some friends
when one said "the
day that's true then
pigs will fly". Just
at that moment I saw
a pig fly past the
window. It seemed
strange but they
never believed me.

Short slippery stories

The
  snake
slithered
silently
  through
    the
      grass
    until
  at
    last
  it
reached
    the
      pond.
        Then
          it
        slipped
    gracefully
into
    the water never to be seen
              again.

Longer stories

To write longer stories it is often best to plan them with chapters:

Chapter One — The Explorers set off
Chapter Two — Danger in the Forest
Chapter Three — Parrot to the Rescue
Chapter Four — In and out of the Quicksand

they were arguing over the last jar of honey. It was so

that he was sailing across the sea in a pea-green

boat with the owl and the pussy-cat

Thoughts

Spare a thought.

We are always having thoughts all the time. Unless we write them down, they are usually lost forever. Of course, it would be impossible and pointless to keep a record of all our thoughts. All the same, writing can be a useful way of helping us to sort out ideas and pin down our more valuable thoughts.

Idle thoughts
Most of us have times when we find ourselves just thinking or day-dreaming. What are your thoughts when you're lying in bed?

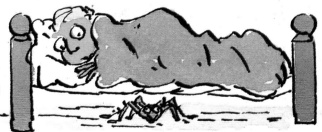

Special thoughts
What are your thoughts about good friends, bedtime, fairies or ghosts?

Remember that it is your own thoughts that make you and your writing special. Hold them carefully. They will take you far.

Writing of writing

Well done all of you who have followed our ways of writing! You have reached the top of the world. You can write of anything for anyone. You can even write of writing.

Writing can be tough
Writing can be fun
Writing can . . . .

And don't forget the magic of spelling,
the treasure of words
and the skills and thrills of grammar.
They won't forget you. They will follow you and assist you wherever you write.

Writers are right. All good writers know that there is always more to explore. They know especially that there is always so much to learn from each other. So keep on travelling – Good wishes to everybody while you *WRITE*, *WRITE* and *WRITE*.

Index